The Art of
Tattoo

Other titles in the *Art Scene* series include:

The Art of Animation
The Art of Anime and Manga
The Art of Comics
The Art of Graffiti
The Art of Graphic Communication

ART SCENE

The Art of
Tattoo

Hal Marcovitz

ReferencePoint
Press®

San Diego, CA

© 2020 ReferencePoint Press, Inc.
Printed in the United States

For more information, contact:
ReferencePoint Press, Inc.
PO Box 27779
San Diego, CA 92198
www.ReferencePointPress.com

LIBRARY OF CONGRESS CATALOGING-IN-PUBLICATION DATA

Names: Marcovitz, Hal, author.
Title: The Art of Tattoo/By Hal Marcovitz.
Description: San Diego, CA: ReferencePoint Press, Inc., [2020] | Series: Art
  Scene | Includes bibliographical references and index. | Audience: Grade 9
  to 12.
Identifiers: LCCN 2019009934 (print) | LCCN 2019012046 (ebook) | ISBN
  9781682825884 (eBook) | ISBN 9781682825877 (hardback)
Subjects: LCSH: Tattooing—History—Juvenile literature. | Tattoo
  artists—Biography—Juvenile literature. | Tattooing—Social
  aspects—Juvenile literature.
Classification: LCC GT2345 (ebook) | LCC GT2345 .M338 2020 (print) | DDC
  391.6/5—dc23
LC record available at https://lccn.loc.gov/2019009934

CONTENTS

Tattoo Art Joins the Mainstream

Although tattoos have been part of human culture for centuries, the art form was not widely practiced in the United States. Even as late as the 1960s, body art in this country was mostly confined to the biceps of sailors and construction workers. Outlaw motorcycle gang members also wore tattoos, often favoring body art that conveyed threatening messages. One familiar tattoo worn by members of the Hells Angels motorcycle gang featured the symbol "1%." The symbol was a reference to a statement issued by the American Motorcyclist Association that contended that 99 percent of motorcycle riders were law-abiding citizens. Therefore, the tattoo worn by the Angels suggested that members of the gang fell among the other 1 percent.

But not all tattoo enthusiasts regarded themselves as roughnecks or lawbreakers. As a young boy, Steve Gilbert, who would go on to serve as an art professor at the University of Toronto in Canada, recalled seeing a tattoo on the arm of his babysitter's boyfriend. Gilbert was impressed by the design and color of the tattoo: a red and green dragon. Later, he told his father about it. "My parents didn't have tattoos, and neither did any of their friends," says Gilbert.

When I told my father about my discovery, he patiently explained that only criminals, savages, and feeble-minded people had tattoos, and that they did it because they didn't have anything better to do. I said I thought tattoos were interesting anyway, and he told me that tattooing seemed interesting to me because I was a child, but that when I grew up I would change my mind. Dad meant well and he was right about a lot of things, but not about that.[1]

Gilbert did not change his mind about tattoos. He became an enthusiastic proponent of tattoo art, getting his first tattoo in 1945 at the age of fourteen—the numeral *13* inked onto his leg—and eventually authoring magazine articles and books about body art. As an artist, he took up the craft himself, applying tattoos to others.

Tattoos of the Stars

Gilbert's enthusiasm for body art was unusual for its time, when tattooing was an art form mostly out of mainstream society. But attitudes started changing in 1970 when Janis Joplin walked into a tattoo studio in San Francisco and asked for a tattoo. At the time, Joplin was one of the top pop music singers in the country. Tattoo artist Lyle Tuttle asked Joplin whether she had any particular design in mind. The singer said she did not, so Tuttle tattooed a pattern resembling a bracelet around her left wrist. Joplin complained that the procedure was more painful than she expected, but she was still dazzled by the result. She asked Tuttle to create a second tattoo. Tuttle complied, tattooing a tiny heart on her left breast—a fitting image, given that two years earlier Joplin had recorded the hit song "Piece of My Heart." Joplin declared the tattoo of the heart was a gift to her male fans. She said, "Just a little treat for the boys. Like icing on the cake."[2]

Joplin is believed to be the first celebrity to openly sport a tattoo, but she would certainly not be the last. Whenever Joplin posed for publicity photos, she showed off her tattoos. Other celebrities took notice, and many soon sought out tattoo artists themselves. For his part, Tuttle created tattoos for pop stars Joan Baez, Jim Croce, and Duane and Greg Allman.

Lady Gaga attends an award show in New York City. Many of today's celebrities have embraced body art, which has helped make tattoos more popular and accepted by society's mainstream.

Today it may be difficult to find a celebrity who is not tattooed. Pop stars such as Justin Bieber, Lady Gaga, Ariana Grande, Miley Cyrus, Zayn Malik, and Adam Levine proudly display their tattoos on stage. The bodies of many major sports stars are covered in tattoos as well, among them basketball stars LeBron James and Carmelo Anthony, football player Chris Long, Ultimate Fighting star Conor McGregor, tennis player Bethanie Mattek-Sands, soccer star Natasha Kai, and Olympic high jumper Inika McPherson. As stars of music and sports perform before audiences that often number in the millions, fans can take notice of the body art that these celebrities proudly wear. And many fans are eager to sport tattoos just like their favorite stars—a factor that has helped propel tattoo art into society's mainstream.

"The styles of tattoo art are as diverse and unique as the individuals wearing them today."[3]

—Joe Capobianco, tattoo artist

Dynamic and Trendsetting

Clearly, celebrities have embraced tattoo art, prompting many of their fans to get their own tattoos. But if the artistic quality of the tattoo had not blossomed over the years as well, body art probably would not have seen the growth in popularity it has achieved since Joplin walked into Tuttle's studio nearly fifty years ago. Joe Capobianco, a tattoo artist in New Haven, Connecticut, believes that "the styles of tattoo art are as diverse and unique as the individuals wearing them today." He says, "It's my thinking that these styles will continue to grow even more diverse and creative as more young and talented artists get into the trade."[3] Indeed, no longer scorned by many members of society, tattoo art is wearable, dynamic, and trendsetting, and it is likely to prompt second looks from all who see it.

CHAPTER ONE

A Modern History of Tattoo Art

By the nineteenth century, tattooing had grown immensely popular in the Asian world. In fact, the English word *tattoo* traces its roots to *tatau*, the Samoan word for body art. In Japan, tattoo artists were known as *horishi*, a word that roughly translates in English to "carver." But in 1872 the Japanese government banned tattooing as immoral. Still, a vast network of underground tattoo artists thrived, thanks mostly to the desire of criminals known as the Yakuza to have their bodies tattooed.

This desire stemmed from several factors. For one, tattooing was illegal, and Yakuza members were always looking for ways to break the law. But it was also painful, which means it took a degree of toughness to submit to the art of the *horishi*. Indeed, the Yakuza were more than willing to flaunt this evidence of their courage. And it was permanent—meaning it marked the wearer for life as a Yakuza. Brian Ashcraft, an author who explores Asian culture, explains:

> When tattoos were outlawed in 1872, anyone who had them was, by default, a criminal. Showing you had tattoos was a way to say, "Hey, I broke the law." This made tattoos look threatening. Even though the ban was lifted after World War II, those connotations remained—and, for many, continue to this day. But as one Japanese tattooist explained, "We must be thankful to the Yakuza for keeping this country's tattoo tradition alive." That's true: When

tattoos were outlawed and tattooists were under the real threat of being arrested for their work, the underworld kept them employed.[4]

Inspired by a Novel

In rendering their art, many Japanese tattoo artists took inspiration from the novel *Suikoden*, which tells the story of Chinese outlaws who challenge an authoritarian regime during the twelfth century. (In English, the novel's title is translated as *The Water Margin*.) Although versions of the novel had been produced in Japan as far back as the 1500s, it was a late-nineteenth-century publication of it that caught the interest of the Yakuza, who appreciated the outlaw ways of the characters and wanted to wear the tattoos described in the text. The readers of the novel were particularly taken with the illustrations by artist Utagawa Kuniyoshi, who sketched the heroes with colorful full-body tattoos. Describing Kuniyoshi's artwork, journalist India Stoughton says,

"Showing you had tattoos was a way to say, 'Hey, I broke the law.' This made tattoos look threatening."[4]

—Brian Ashcraft, author

> One of the most popular of Kuniyoshi's 75 illustrations . . . depicts a scene from a story about a former fisherman and smuggler named Ruan Xiaowu who, with his two brothers, joined the bandits of Mount Liang. His tattoo of a fierce leopard, which is described in the original novel, is shown . . . peeking out from under subtle monochrome patterns that evoke the animal's pelt and cover the hero's entire back, as he engages in a dramatic underwater fight with an enemy general intent on capturing the bandits.[5]

Among the images inked onto the bodies of the Yakuza were mythical beasts such as dragons as well as real-life

Utagawa Kuniyoshi's illustrations, such as this nineteenth-century woodcut of a warrior with full-body tattoos, inspired the Yakuza and horishi *to explore bold, colorful tattoos that covered large portions of the body.*

ferocious animals, including snakes, leopards, and tigers. The *horishi* also exhibited a lighter touch, rendering images of flowers and friendly birds. Moreover, their work was colorful. And perhaps most significantly, the *horishi* did not limit their work to the biceps of their clients. They regarded the full body as their canvas, extending their art from the neck to the heel. As Ashcraft says, "The full body suits, with their intricate designs and elaborate backgrounds, must have looked like artistic marvels to foreigners. No wonder they influenced a generation of talented Western tattooers."[6] Indeed, the body art created by the *horishi* has influenced tattoo artists well into the twenty-first century.

Tattooing in the Bowery

The full-body tattoos rendered by the *horishi* may have been popular among the Yakuza, but it would take another century before tattoo clients in the West would be comfortable with the notion of being permanently inked virtually from head to toe. In the late 1800s tattoo artists in America were confronted with a much different type of clientele. Tattoo studios were typically located in port cities, and their clients were invariably sailors on leave who made their way into town with pockets full of cash, thanks to the ship's paymaster. Sailors landing in New York Harbor found what they needed in the city neighborhood known as the Bowery and, in particular, in the Bowery's Chatham Square.

At the time, Chatham Square was the center of a bustling New York nightlife with dozens of saloons, gambling houses, theaters, burlesque halls, and tattoo studios, all located within an area of a few blocks. One of those studios was owned by tattoo artist Samuel O'Reilly, who was so busy rendering tattoos for sailors and other customers that he found himself unable to keep up with the demand.

O'Reilly accommodated his clients as best he could, but like other tattoo artists of the time, he was limited by the rudimentary tools available to him. These tools consisted of needles attached to wooden handles. The artist dipped the needle tips into ink, then used the needles to puncture the skin of the client. Working slowly, the artist spent hours fashioning the tattoo into the layer of skin known as the dermis. The dermis is the second layer of skin, about 0.125 inches (3 mm) below the top layer, known as the epidermis. The dermis, which is about 0.08 inches (2 mm) in thickness, is much softer than the epidermis, so it is able to absorb the ink of the tattoo needle. Therefore, the tattoo artist needs to first puncture the tough epidermis, then push the ink into the dermis.

O'Reilly knew that he could earn a higher income if he could work more rapidly—the faster he could complete a tattoo, the faster he could seat the next client in his chair. In 1891 he searched for a machine that could help speed up the tattoo process, and he soon discovered an apparatus known as the electric pen.

Edison's Electric Pen

The device had been developed sixteen years earlier by Thomas Edison, one of history's preeminent inventors, responsible for producing such innovations as the electric light bulb, the movie camera, the phonograph, and the alkaline battery. As he tinkered in his laboratory in West Orange, New Jersey, it is unlikely Edison envisioned the impact the electric pen would have on tattoo art over the course of the next century.

The device, which was connected to a source of electricity, shot a jolt of current through the brass barrel of the pen. Inside the barrel was a cam—essentially a slide that moved up and down. At the end of the cam was a needle. The cam moved the needle quickly in an in-and-out motion, enabling the user to cut through a sheet of paper, creating a stencil. By placing a clean sheet of paper beneath the stencil, then rolling ink over the stencil, the user could make a copy of what he or she had just written—or, certainly, dozens of copies. Edison received a patent for the electric pen in 1876. It was mostly used by office workers to make duplicates of their correspondence.

O'Reilly modified the electric pen, replacing the machine's needles with tattoo needles. By using the new machine, tattoo

Tattoos and the Circus

During the nineteenth century and the early years of the twentieth, it was rare to find people in America and Europe wearing full-body tattoos. Mostly, tattoo clients such as sailors and assorted roughnecks wanted no more than their biceps tattooed. But anybody who visited the circus in those years was virtually guaranteed to see a man or woman wearing full-body tattoos. These men and women had their bodies tattooed to earn livings as circus performers.

One of the most famous of the tattooed women of the era was a performer known as La Belle Irene, whose body was decorated by tattoo machine inventor Samuel O'Reilly. As art professor and tattoo historian Steve Gilbert recounts, "La Belle Irene . . . made her London debut in 1890, claiming to be the first completely tattooed woman ever exhibited in a circus. Her decorations included an artistic assortment of flowers, birds, hearts, cupids, scrolls and sentimental inscriptions borrowed from the ornamental commercial art of the day."

Following World War II, the practice of exhibiting tattooed men and women in the circus all but died out. They had been performers in what were commonly known as freak shows, which also featured performers who had been placed on exhibit to showcase their physical oddities, such as morbid obesity, dwarfism, or unusual height. By then, the public had come to view freak shows as demeaning to the performers, and circus owners responded by eliminating the shows.

Steve Gilbert, *Tattoo History: A Sourcebook*. New York: Juno, 2000, pp. 135–36.

artists could insert, withdraw, and reinsert the needle into the dermis at a much faster pace because the needle was now propelled by an electric charge. In fact, O'Reilly's machine was capable of making up to fifty punctures per minute—much quicker than an artist could accomplish with just his or her fingers to manipulate the tattoo needle. (Today's tattoo machines, which are still based on the concept of the electric pen but have undergone significant technological advances since O'Reilly's time, are capable of making up to 3,000 punctures per minute.)

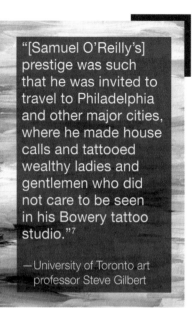

In 1891 O'Reilly received his own patent for his new tattoo machine. His business boomed to the degree that he had to hire other tattoo artists to help keep up with the demand in his Bowery studio. "Tattooing in the US was revolutionized overnight," says Steve Gilbert. "O'Reilly was swamped with orders and made a small fortune within a few years. His prestige was such that he was invited to travel to Philadelphia and other major cities, where he made house calls and tattooed wealthy ladies and gentlemen who did not care to be seen in his Bowery tattoo studio."[7]

Alberts Introduces Flash Art

Thanks to O'Reilly's tattoo machine, by the 1930s the tattoo business in the Bowery was thriving. The clients were still mainly sailors on leave who, when they walked into a tattoo studio, had specific designs in mind. Most clients of the era wanted their biceps emblazoned with images of the American eagle or similar patriotic symbols. Female images, such as pinup girls or hula dancers, were also popular. And even though studios were now equipped with tattoo machines, artists still looked for efficient ways to get their clients in their seats, tattooed, and out the door as soon as possible so the next client could be seated. As a result of these factors, the designs offered to clients were decidedly simple, which enabled the artists to render the images quickly.

Still, there were tattoo artists working in the Bowery who took their art seriously. One such artist was Lew Alberts, a former wallpaper designer who regarded his work as a cut above that of the typical tattoo practitioner of the era. True, he fulfilled his clients' desires for patriotic images and pinup girls across their biceps, but his images were much more pronounced and more finely detailed than the typical designs of the day. His lines and colors were bolder. He took the time to render shadows. His characters did not wear blank expressions but rather friendly smiles, cheeky grins, and frowns. Alberts confided to friends that many of his designs were inspired from books he had seen depicting the Japanese-style tattoos favored by the Yakuza. As tattoo artist Don Ed Hardy recalls, Alberts "was educated and articulate, and he showed me a book of Japanese tattooing. When I saw that, I thought, 'Oh, my God, if tattoos can look like that, I think I want to do this.'"[8]

Alberts was the first tattoo artist to create what is known as flash art, which comprises colored sketches of tattoos rendered onto paper, then posted on the walls of tattoo studios. Flash art meant that a client could walk into the studio and pick out a design he or she wanted simply by finding a favorite flash on the

A sailor gets a tattoo in a Boston tattoo parlor in the early 1940s. Most clients at that time in the United States were sailors on leave who chose tattoos of patriotic symbols.

wall. Flash art also sped up business. A client could now select a flash within a few seconds instead of spending several minutes in a dialogue with the artist, describing the design he or she wanted.

Stencil Art

Not only did Alberts enhance his own business by using flash art, he established a lucrative trade by selling his flash to other tattoo artists. Eventually, a bustling market in flash was created in the tattoo world as artists bought, sold, and traded flash art among themselves. Today, flash art remains a common element in the tattoo

Ötzi and the Ice Princess

Humans had been receiving tattoos for centuries before the *horishi* got down to work. In fact, the first humans to have received tattoos may have gotten their body art some five thousand years ago.

In 1991 hikers making their way across the Austrian Alps came across the mummified body of a man later determined to have lived in approximately 3200 BCE. Scientists named him Ötzi because he was found in an Alpine region known as Ötztal.

Ötzi's body was well preserved. Evidently, he had been encased in ice since his death. Scientists examining his body counted fifty-nine separate tattoos. Whoever applied the tattoos had used charcoal instead of ink. Mostly, the scientists found crosses and slashes on Ötzi's ankles, wrists, knees, back, and chest. However, it is unknown whether the tattoos were applied by an artist or by a physician of the era. Scientists have theorized that the tattoos may not have been decorative; instead, they may have been the result of treatments similar to acupuncture. Therefore, the incisions could have been made to treat ailments Ötzi suffered. Nevertheless, the charcoal-colored marks decorating Ötzi's body remained intact, making him history's first-known tattoo client.

Two years later, the body of a woman also encased in ice was unearthed in a region of Russia known as Ukok. Scientists called her the Ice Princess and estimated that she lived during the fifth century BCE. Unlike Ötzi's tattoos, the patterns on the Ice Princess's body form definite images, among them a deer and a panther.

business, although flash is more likely to be found on a tattoo artist's website or Instagram account rather than tacked to studio walls.

As flash art became more common, so did stencils. Before injecting the ink into the dermis, the artist must first render the design across the client's epidermis to act as a guide before the tattoo needles are employed. But sketching the design freehand takes time, using up valuable minutes that could better be used in actually injecting the ink into the dermis. The stencil saved time. When the client walked into the studio, the design he or she selected from the choice of flash art had already been rendered onto a stencil. All the artist needed to do was press the stencil into the flesh, transferring the ink onto the epidermis.

At first, tattoo artists used stencils drawn on ordinary sketch paper, but these tended to fall apart after just a few uses. Artists turned next to acetate stencils. Acetate is a clear, thin plastic sheet, much sturdier than paper. Starting in the 1980s, tattoo artists have used papers specially developed for stencils. Moreover, for clients who prefer original images not available in the studio's inventory of flash art, special copy machines have been developed that can quickly transfer a design made on ordinary sketch paper onto the tattoo stencil paper.

The Birth of the Tattoo Renaissance

Although the tools of the trade had drastically changed since O'Reilly's early days, the clientele for tattoos had not. Even as late as the 1960s, sailors were still very important customers, and construction workers and outlaw bikers had also become frequent clients.

Some tattoo artists realized that if their trade was ever to expand beyond these clients, the artwork had to evolve beyond the typical designs. Since the earliest days of tattooing, no formal training in art had ever been a prerequisite for a tattoo artist to find a job. Over the years, an informal system of apprenticeship had been developed—most artists learned by working in the studios of other artists. But during the 1960s and 1970s, a new class of

19

tattoo artists started joining the field. These artists were graduates of university fine arts programs, and they brought their skills and ideas of what constituted art to the tattoo trade. They helped launch the modern renaissance in tattoo art.

Among the important tattoo artists of the era was Cliff Raven of Chicago. Raven held a degree in fine art from Indiana University. He drew inspiration from Greek mythology, tattooing his clients with images of minotaurs (half-man, half-bull monsters), winged serpents, and similar creatures. Raven also moved his tattoos beyond his clients' biceps, enlarging them so they covered their entire backs. Some images were even larger, starting behind the neck and snaking down the client's legs to the ankle. Raven's designs were very much inspired by those rendered by the full-body artists in Japan. As tattoo historian Anna Felicity Friedman explains, "Although traditional . . . tattooing has persisted, the dramatic new tattoo styles and techniques that came out of the tattoo renaissance spread across the United States to Europe and beyond, forming the foundations for the great diversity of global tattooing today."[9]

Embraced by Young Adults

Raven and other tattoo artists from the 1960s and 1970s helped widen the interest in tattoos beyond sailors, bikers, and construction workers to younger clients. Statistics support the notion that young adults have robustly embraced tattoo art. According to a 2017 study by the Pew Research Center, a Washington, DC, polling organization, 38 percent of people between the ages of eighteen and twenty-nine—some 20 million Americans—have at least one tattoo. A similar poll conducted in 2012 by the Canadian polling firm Ipsos Reid found that 36 percent of Canadians between the ages of eighteen and twenty-four—about 2.6 million—have at least one tattoo. Moreover, Friedman estimates that the number of people in the United States and Canada earning their livings as professional tattoo artists is in the tens of thousands. Friedman

Today's young people have embraced tattoo art and culture. Some 20 million Americans between the ages of eighteen and twenty-nine have at least one tattoo.

contends that "tattooing became hip because of its boundary-pushing perception, especially among college students."[10]

And so, over the decades of the nineteenth, twentieth, and twenty-first centuries, tattoo art emerged from the shadows in Japan, where it was illegal but nevertheless embraced by the outlaws known as the Yakuza. The art of tattoo made its way into the back-alley Bowery shops, where artists implemented technological innovations not to enhance the art but as a way to get more clients in and out of their businesses. Finally, though, tattoo art has undergone a renaissance in which the true talents of the artists are being displayed on the bodies of clients who now welcome the notion of being inked virtually from head to toe.

> "Tattooing became hip because of its boundary-pushing perception, especially among college students."[10]
>
> —Anna Felicity Friedman, tattoo historian

CHAPTER TWO

Tattoo Artists of Influence

Tattoo art has come a long way since the era of the Bowery artists, who were mostly concerned with creating quick, simple images on the biceps of sailors on shore leave. In recent years a true renaissance has swept over the world of tattoo. Highly skilled artists have transformed their clients' bodies into living canvases. Several of these artists are recognized as leaders of the tattoo renaissance. Sailor Jerry Collins, for instance, saw the potential of full-body tattoos. Filip Leu helped make this concept possible by developing new needles that could cover larger portions of the human body. Eva Karabudak helped raise the standard of the form by rendering interpretations of some of the world's most famous works of art. Yomico Moreno applied the concept of realism to tattoo art, rendering tattoos that resemble photographs. And Amanda Wachob offered an abstract interpretation of images and their application.

Sailor Jerry Collins: Full-Body Pioneer

Born Norman Keith Collins in 1911, Collins earned the nickname "Sailor Jerry" thanks largely to the years he spent in the US Navy during the 1930s, traveling mostly throughout Asia. Before enlisting in the navy, Collins worked at a tattoo studio in Chicago, learning the craft from tattoo artist Gib "Tatts" Thomas. Given the degree of training he received, it may be difficult to see how Collins could envision tattooing as an art. To further hone his skills beyond what he learned in Thomas's studio, Collins practiced on people who were living on Chicago's skid row. He paid them a few cents each to let him tattoo their bodies. He also had a friend in the city morgue who allowed him to tattoo the corpses of unfortunate city denizens found by police, still awaiting relatives to claim their remains.

Sailor Jerry (pictured is a sample of his flash art) was inspired by the body art he saw in Asia while serving in the US Navy. He incorporated the vivid, intricate style of Japanese tattoo artists in his own work but had a definite American touch.

designed by
SAILOR JERRY

designed by
SAILOR JERRY

Following World War II, Collins opened his own tattoo shop in Honolulu, Hawaii. In 1960 Collins began to move away from tattoos on biceps, instead creating full-body expressions of art. This concept was, of course, nothing new: The full-body tattoo was common in Japan; during Collins's travels as a sailor, he had seen Japanese citizens wearing these tattoos. The full-body tattoos Collins rendered for his clients, however, were drawn with a definite American touch. Collins's clients wore tattoo depictions of General George Armstrong Custer's battle at the Little Big Horn, the battle for the Alamo in Texas, and patriots fighting the British during the Revolutionary War. Of course, hula girls, mermaids, skulls, and daggers were also common figures in Collins's work — as they were among the works of most tattoo artists of the era. Nevertheless, it was Collins who envisioned the full body as the canvas for American tattoo artists.

Collins died in 1973, but decades later his work continues to inspire tattoo artists and others who follow tattoo culture. "He's credited as being one of the first tattoo artists that blended the nuances and coloring and storytelling of the Japanese masters with the bold line look and topics of American tattooing," says Erich Weiss, a Philadelphia filmmaker who produced a 2009 documentary about Collins. "He took pieces of American history and tied them in."[11]

Filip Leu Revolutionizes the Needle

By the time Filip Leu was born in Paris in 1967, his parents, Felix and Loretta Leu, were already professional tattoo artists. When the Leus opened their tattoo studio in Lausanne, Switzerland, in 1982, Filip and his siblings joined the family business.

Eventually, Filip Leu found that his clients were demanding larger and larger tattoos. No longer content to see their images confined to biceps, wrists, or shoulders, clients wanted to see their tattoos extended across large swathes of their bodies. At the time, this was difficult to accomplish for the simple reason

Cross-Stitching with Eva Karabudak

Although she has earned renown in the tattoo world for her reproductions of great works of art, Eva Karabudak, also known as Eva Krbdk, first caught the attention of tattoo aficionados when she developed what is known as the cross-stitching style of tattoo. Cross-stitching is a technique employed in sewing using stitches in the form of the letter *X* and different colors of thread in a pattern that produces a recognizable image such as a bird or flower.

Instead of using thread, Karabudak uses ink, making tiny *X*'s in the skin to create the pattern. Karabudak says cross-stitching has proved to be popular because many of her clients owned items that had been cross-stitched by a grandmother or other relative when they were children. "I used to do cross-stitch on canvas and cloth at home and decided to do tattoos out of it," says Karabudak. "It's an anchor back to a lot of people's childhoods. That's why I believe it gets noticed."

The website Bored Panda comments,

> Many people consider cross-stitching to be something their grand-ma would do, but Eva Krbdk . . . seems to think otherwise. Her cross-stitch tattoo designs look like a cross between pixel art and the popular folk art they're named for. Many of her pieces are simple and cute, but with a large-enough canvas, they can become truly impressive, utilizing a wide array of colors that blend to form beautiful images.

Quoted in Emily Laurence, "A Stitch in Time," *Metro*, July 20, 2015. www.metro.us.

Bored Panda, "Cross-Stitch Tattoos by Turkish Artist Eva Krbdk," 2019. www.boredpanda.com.

that the technology of the tattoo machine had not yet caught up with the artistic developments in the medium of tattoo. The needles employed by the artists were too finely milled, meaning most tattoos were rendered with lines no wider than what a pencil could make on a sheet of paper. This meant that it could take several days, if not weeks, to produce a tattoo across a client's back, or down the entire length of a leg, or even across a large section of skin. In addition, the longer tattooing sessions meant the clients had to endure longer episodes of pain as the artists worked.

In the early 2000s, Leu started designing his own needles, some with points as wide as 0.18 inches (0.45 mm). By contrast, the point of a typical tattoo needle measures 0.01 inches (0.30 mm). The thicker points enabled Leu to render thicker lines on his clients' skin, meaning he could speed up the process of creating large tattoos.

But Leu had to do more than simply widen the needle points. The machine itself needed to be reengineered. With wider needles, the sleeves holding the needles had to be widened, and the electric charges pulsating through the needles also had to be altered because wider needles required more voltage. As Clinton R. Sanders, a professor of sociology at Northwestern University in Evanston, Illinois, and a longtime student of tattoo culture, explains, "The end result . . . was revolutionary for tattoo artists working in large scale since it allowed the artist to complete a full backpiece in as little as 12 hours, with less damage to the skin and substantially less pain for the client."[12]

"I went to Japan when I was seventeen for the first time and I got to see all these men with bodysuits in real life. It was very beautiful."[13]

—Filip Leu, tattoo artist

In addition to making these innovations, Leu was well prepared for the full-body movement that would take over the tattoo world during the 2000s. He had studied tattooing in Japan, where full-body tattoos had been common since the early era of the Yakuza. Leu says, "I went to Japan when I was seventeen for the first time and I got to see all these men with bodysuits in real life. It was very beautiful. I like Japanese [tattooing] because it is so graphic. What I also like about it is that it is one design. The back is the center, and the arms and the legs are the accompaniment. It's a complete work."[13]

The Fine Art of Eva Karabudak

Eva Karabudak, a tattoo artist based in New York City, draws her inspiration directly from fine works of art. Karabudak—who is

Acclaimed tattoo artist Eva Karabudak draws inspiration from the fine arts, often re-creating scenes from famous paintings in her tattoos, such as Gustav Klimt's The Kiss.

also known as Eva Krbdk—specializes in small tattoos rendered in geometric shapes, such as circles or squares. Within those shapes, Karabudak reproduces some of the world's most famous paintings, including works by Vincent Van Gogh, known for his colorful landscapes and still lifes, and Gustav Klimt, famous for his portraiture.

Born in Turkey, Karabudak majored in art at Gazi University in Ankara. She spent her free time creating artistic graffiti, but she soon turned to tattoo art. Her first job after receiving her art degree was as a tattoo artist in a small shop in Ankara. She later opened her own tattoo studio in the Turkish city of Istanbul.

Tattoos in Museums

Although tattoos are now regarded by many experts as a form of fine art, most museums have yet to find ways to stage true exhibitions of tattoo art. A main reason is that tattoos, in their truest form, are worn by living people who cannot practically be formed into a long-running, static museum exhibition. Therefore, whenever museums have staged exhibits of tattoo art, they have usually featured photographs of tattoos or mannequins decorated with tattoo-like images.

In 2015 the New Museum in New York collaborated with Amanda Wachob to provide a live exhibit of tattoo art. Over a period of six weeks, Wachob rendered tattoos onto twelve volunteers who were chosen from applications they submitted prior to the show, which was titled *Skin Data*. Moreover, as Wachob rendered the tattoos onto the volunteers, abstract re-creations of her images were projected onto an overhead screen in the museum. The images were generated by the pulses of electricity running through the tattoo machine, displaying streaks and splashes of color as Wachob worked.

In addition, the images created by electric pulses were captured by a computer, then rendered onto paper and made available for sale in the museum store. Henri Neuendorf, an associate editor of the website Artnet, writes that "the visual representation of tattoos in the form of a print challenges the perceptions of contemporary art as well as body art and explores how technology can be utilized to blur the lines between performance, tattoo, and fine art."

Henri Neuendorf, "New Museum Makes Push to Classify Tattoos as Art," Artnet, December 12, 2014. https://news.artnet.com.

In 2016 Karabudak moved to New York City. After arriving in the United States, Karabudak developed her distinctive tattoo style of replicating famous works of art. Her tattoos have featured *The Birth of Venus* by fifteenth-century Italian artist Sandro Botticelli, depicting the goddess standing on a huge seashell; Van Gogh's *Starry Night*, showing a landscape of colorful, circular starbursts; and Klimt's *The Kiss*, depicting a couple embracing, clothed in silver and gold robes. Her work has found an international following; by 2019, her Instagram account reported nearly six hundred thousand followers.

Karabudak has continued to broaden her tattoo portfolio. In addition to famous works of art, she also draws inspiration from storybooks and movie scenes and creates original images as well. As Alex Wikoff, a staff writer for the website Tattoodo, notes,

> Predominantly circular in nature, her tiny works often feature landscapes or idyllic scenery, most of which lack any distinct border, and seem to float atop the skin, creating the illusion that perhaps the piece has been painted on with acrylics instead of tattooed. Painterly and precise, her tattoos often call on movie scenes, famous paintings, and the occasional [original] image as inspiration.[14]

Yomico Moreno: Tattoo Realist

Realism is a common genre in the art world. Artists who practice realism present a scene on canvas exactly as it would appear in real life—as though they used a camera to create the picture rather than palettes of oil paints or watercolors. These images are often gritty and, at times, unpleasant to see because they may reflect life in its harshest moments. Nevertheless, artists who adhere to the rules of realism do not attempt to beautify their images by making their subjects more attractive to the eye than they really are.

Although realism is rare in the tattoo world, it is becoming more common thanks to the art of Yomico Moreno, who is regarded as one of the premier practitioners of realism. His tattoos appear to be more like photographs printed on his clients' skin than inked sketches. The portraits he creates feature deep shadows under the eyes, unshaven faces with the stubble of early beards, and the wrinkled skin of the elderly. Close-ups of eyes depict the red lines of sleeplessness. A tattoo of a scar drips with blood-like red ink. His renderings of spiders, scorpions, and cockroaches seem almost alive.

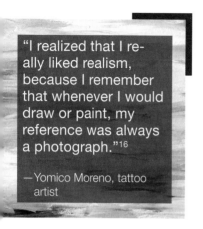

One of Moreno's favorite tattoos is a thick yellow snake, inked as though it coils around a client's forearm. Viewers can see the snake's scales rippling across the curves and indentations in the creature's body. At the end of the image, the tip of the snake's tail is lifted subtly, producing a tiny shadow. To render the original snake tattoo, Moreno says he did not simply close his eyes and envision the animal; rather, he spent hours reading about snakes and studying photographs of the reptiles in the wild. "This one was a big challenge because I had to anatomically study many pictures of snakes to get that texture, to give the impression of something quite real,"[15] Moreno explains.

Moreno says he sacrificed a lot for his art, at first turning down clients who wanted him to tattoo typical depictions of skulls and fairy-tale dragons. He recalls,

I realized that I really liked realism, because I remember that whenever I would draw or paint, my reference was always a photograph. . . . I went a long time without work, but after some time, someone came to me for a portrait, and this portrait brought about more portraits. It was a sacrifice that I had to make many years ago, but now I know that it was a good decision, because it was the only way that I was able to show people my style.[16]

Born in Puerto Cabello, Venezuela, Moreno eventually joined the renowned New York City studio Last Rites Tattoo Theatre, where the waiting list for his tattoo art can be as long as eight months.

Amanda Wachob's Abstract Art

Not all tattoo artists are drawn to realism. Today many of them work in a more abstract style. Abstract art does not attempt to provide a realistic image of a scene but rather allows the artist to interpret the scene using his or her own emotions as a guide. Therefore, the artist can alter light, color, outline, or any other aspect of the scene to conform to the way he or she sees it. The most dramatic form of abstract art is known as abstract expressionism, in which seemingly random streaks and dabs of paint are used to depict an image.

Amanda Wachob is perhaps the tattoo world's best-known abstract artist. After studying photography at the State University of New York at Purchase, Wachob decided to pursue a career in tattooing. In 1998 she found a job at a small studio

Renowned tattoo artist Amanda Wachob works on a tattoo during an exhibition of her art at the Museum of Contemporary Art Denver. One of Wachob's specialties is using free-flowing splashes of colors in her tattoos to create abstract images.

in the town of Kingston, New York. It was there that Wachob developed her distinctive style—beginning by simply asking her clients whether she could refrain from outlining the images on their skin in black ink. That is how most tattoos are rendered. Deep, crisp black outlines help define the image, and colors—or shades of gray—fill in the outlines. "I just thought it would be interesting to approach tattooing from the perspective of painting," she says.

> So much of tattooing is about drawing, and it's heavily based on illustrations. You're using pencils and making sketches and drawings. . . . So say, if somebody came to me and asked for a tulip, I would say, "I could do this with a black outline or I can do this without, if you just want the color." It didn't make sense to me why for certain tattoos there had to be a black outline; not everybody wanted something that looked like a cartoon.[17]

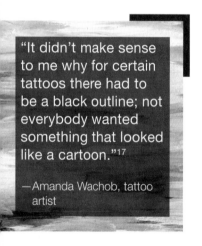

"It didn't make sense to me why for certain tattoos there had to be a black outline; not everybody wanted something that looked like a cartoon."[17]

—Amanda Wachob, tattoo artist

Wachob's other specialty is using free-flowing splashes of color to help compose abstract images. Clients have their bodies decorated with dabs of color rendered in swirls, curlicues, and streaks. Sometimes, the dabs of tattoo ink form portraits or other images, such as flowers, but oftentimes the abstraction of the scene has taken completely over, and the tattoo is composed of seemingly random streaks, dots, curves, and lines. That was the style of tattoo Wachob applied to the shoulder of journalist Drew Grant—in Grant's case, a splash of red circles and black strokes. In 2012 Grant attended the annual Christmas party at the White House. As she was mingling with the dignitaries in attendance, Grant felt a tap on her shoulder. She turned, coming face-to-face with President Barack Obama. "I like your tattoo,"[18] he told her.

Wachob works out of her own studio in New York City. In 2019 her website reported that her appointments were booked more than a year in advance. Her Instagram followers number more than 120,000.

Wachob, Collins, Leu, Karabudak, and Moreno have brought different styles to the art of tattoo, but they are all key members of an artistic community that has helped make tattoos into the full-body expressions of art that they are today. They have all participated in the renaissance that helped establish tattoos as an art form for creative people in the twenty-first century.

CHAPTER THREE

Inspirations Behind Tattoo Art

Fans of the *Alien* series of films are well acquainted with the work of the late Swiss painter H.R. Giger. He conceived the images of the hideous, blood-curdling aliens that have populated the films since the 1970s, terrorizing space explorers as well as colonists on distant planets. By 2017, six films had been produced in the series, earning more than $1 billion in worldwide box office revenue. As many as three sequels are planned for the future. In addition, numerous comic books, novels, and no fewer than eighteen video games have been spawned by the film series.

Norwegian tattoo artist Rico Schinkel is a big fan of the *Alien* films and, in particular, the work of Giger. In fact, much of Schinkel's tattoo work is inspired by Giger. Schinkel's clients often leave his tattoo studio bearing images of snarling, fanged extraterrestrial creatures. In addition to aliens, Giger was also fascinated with biomechanical imagery—in other words, linking the bodies of living creatures with robotic arms, legs, or other mechanical body parts. Schinkel has created similar imagery, applying it to the skin of his clients. "You can combine biomechanical with everything,"[19] he suggests. Many of the characters in Schinkel's tattoos are fearsome creatures with mechanical faces; others have metallic claws extending from their hands. One Schinkel tattoo features an image of the seventeenth-century British dissident Guy Fawkes; he is smiling devilishly but has a clock protruding from his forehead.

The days when tattoo art was dominated by images such as bald eagles and hula dancers are long gone. Tattoo artists no longer confine themselves to such simple images. Their work is far more complicated and artistic and is based on inspirations that go well beyond the drawings found on the tattoo flash produced during the era of Lew Alberts. Many tattoo artists are graduates of prestigious art schools and are anxious to put their talents to work creating innovative images for their clients. Moreover, many clients seek out the top talent in tattoo art because they desire an original, artistic design. "Personally, I hate anything without imagination or mystery," says British tattoo artist Cyle Hoffman, "such as tattoos related to football, patriotism, song lyrics and names. I will turn them down and lose money rather than do them."[20]

> "Personally, I hate anything without imagination or mystery, such as tattoos related to football, patriotism, song lyrics and names. I will turn them down and lose money rather than do them."[20]
>
> —Cyle Hoffman, tattoo artist

Birds and Butterflies

Because his work is influenced by Giger, much of Schinkel's images are dark and sinister. Certainly, though, other tattoo artists find inspiration in much more pleasant ideas. In fact, much of Riki-Kay Middleton's work is inspired by a far different type of artist: Albrecht Dürer. Working during the late fifteenth and early sixteenth centuries, the German artist won renown as a painter, but he was also a pioneering book illustrator. Dürer illustrated books using the art of the woodcut. This involves carving detailed images into blocks of wood, which are then inked and pressed into the paper to produce the images featured on the pages of the books. Dürer produced woodcut images of knights on horseback, members of noble families, angels taking wing, scenes from the Bible, and numerous varieties of animals, ranging from a rhinoceros and a lion to rabbits, birds, and monkeys.

"I remember the day I discovered this huge vintage book about Albrecht Dürer," says Middleton, whose tattoo studio is located in the city of Guelph, Ontario. "The moment I saw his

35

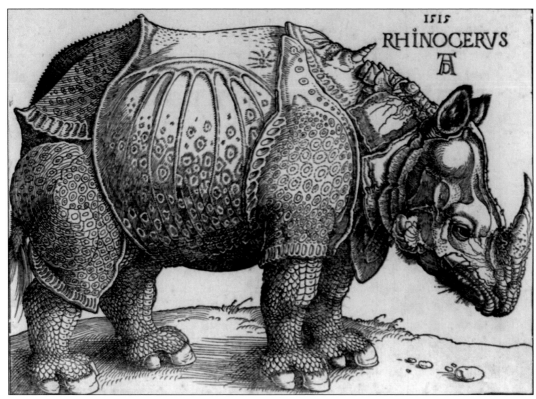

Tattoo artists often draw inspiration from the art world. The Canadian artist Riki-Kay Middleton began emulating the technique of German artist Albrecht Dürer (pictured is a woodcut by Dürer) after discovering a book of his engravings.

work it just felt right. Right away I started emulating his techniques but with a pen rather than woodcuts, and eventually developed my own style."[21] Like Dürer's woodcuts, Middleton's tattoos are created primarily with black ink. Her clients are often tattooed with friendly images of flowers, rabbits, cats, and birds. One Middleton image shows a deer wearing a garland of flowers on its head. Other common works rendered by Middleton include butterflies spreading their wings across her clients' bodies.

Bold Lettering

The tattoos created by artists such as Middleton and Schinkel are inspired by the works of traditional artists. Wilmington, Delaware, tattoo artist B.J. Betts finds his inspiration in an art form with roots in the past as well. In his case, though, the art takes the form of lettering, also known in the tattoo world as script.

Betts is fascinated with the many different fonts, also known as typefaces, that have been created over the centuries. While Betts may tattoo portraits, clock faces, flowers, and other images, most of his work also includes lettering carrying messages desired by his clients. His tattoos often include bold lettering, inked in a number of different typefaces. A favorite font is Old

Inspired by the Past

Tattoos of hula dancers, mermaids, screaming skulls, American eagles, and similar images that dominated tattoo art in the past are not necessarily extinct. At the Old World Tattoo Parlour in Newport, Oregon, husband and wife tattoo artists Aaron and Dana Dixon specialize in the style of tattoos that were popular decades ago. Dana says she finds inspiration in the images created by Sailor Jerry Collins and his contemporaries. "I have a sense of duty to keep their work alive," she says.

There is no question, though, that the tattoos rendered by the Dixons are created with significantly more artistic skill than what could have been expected in the Bowery studios of the last century. The Dixons' flash art shows intricate lines and shadows, colors that range from subtle shades to incandescent hues, and characters who wear bright and cheery expressions rather than the dour grimaces often favored by the Bowery artists. Aaron's flash work includes a variety of ship anchors—popular with the former sailors on shore leave—as well as numerous styles of snakes and serpents wrapping themselves around daggers. Mermaids, eagles, and panthers also find their way into his designs. Meanwhile, Dana renders images of hula dancers as well as mermaids, but snarling skeletons and colorful peacocks also adorn the bodies of her clients. According to tattoo historian Anna Felicity Friedman, "[Dana] Dixon's work combines a strong respect for tattoo work of the past with her own thoughtful sensibility."

Quoted in Anna Felicity Friedman, *The World Atlas of Tattoo*. New Haven, CT: Yale University Press, 2015, p. 45.

Friedman, *The World Atlas of Tattoo*, p. 45.

English, which features grand, thickly inked letters and prominent serifs, which are the projections at the ends of the strokes that compose the letters. He also favors fonts resembling calligraphy, the fancy penmanship that is rendered by hand. Betts may even decorate the letters themselves, inking flowers and stems that entwine them. Since the lettering is an important element of Betts's tattoos, he makes sure it stands out: he tattoos it in stark black ink.

In fact, tattoos emblazoned with lettering are hardly new. For decades, many visitors to the tattoo shops in the Bowery left with the names of their girlfriends tattooed across their biceps or chests. And other tattoos feature the word *Mother*. But Betts says those old-style Bowery tattoos, and the lettering used for them, hardly illustrated the artistic possibilities of lettered tattoos. Indeed, he says, much thought has to go into the lettering so that

Bold lettering has appeared in tattoo art from the early Bowery days, but today's script is much more sophisticated and refined, enhancing the image and helping to tell its story.

the fonts fit the messages of the tattoos as well as the images that will be rendered alongside the script. Also, much thought needs to be given to the places on the body where the tattoos will appear. For example, he says, a font that appears as though it is handwritten will not work if it is rendered vertically, perhaps down the side of the leg. "[It] doesn't look good going down—with stacked letters—it just won't look cool," Betts says. He adds,

> If you're getting a portrait, you don't want gang-banger lettering. All the shapes need to fit the whole feel of the tattoo. If you want your stomach done (for example) you might want it to look hard. You want the lettering to "wow" and look a little gangster. It needs to fit the look you want to accomplish. . . .
>
> Tattoo lettering needs to portray the feeling you want for your tattoo. The right font will do that. Additionally, don't get carried away with ornament. . . . The lettering needs to read clearly, just like any tattoo. Again, don't get caught up in the unnecessary. The approach to lettering is like a drawing, make sure it is clear and legible. Make sure the letters you choose have the basic structure they need for legibility.[22]

Dizzy Elephants and Laughing Dinosaurs

Tattoo artists like Betts, who specialize in lettering, practice an extremely challenging form of tattoo art. Not all tattoo artists are comfortable creating script on their clients' bodies—and few do it well. According to *Inked* magazine, "The uninitiated may believe that tattooing script should be one of the easiest things to accomplish, but let it be known that many of the most renowned artists in the world have a hard time doing lettering. On the surface lettering seems to be simple but in reality there is a ton of artistry and skill that needs to be used to create the perfect script tattoo."[23]

Like Betts, Jessica Weichers provides script in her tattoos, but her fonts are far simpler than what Betts may offer, mostly because the messages have less impact. The script style Weichers mostly uses resembles neat and careful handwriting. The messages in the script Weichers renders in her studio in Festus, a small town near St. Louis, Missouri, may simply display brief romantic notes or perhaps the names of girlfriends, boyfriends, spouses, or children. Weichers tattoos in reds, pinks, blues, greens—whatever hues fit the image. Her choices of colors make sense for her tattoos because she says she is mostly inspired by fairy tales and other stories for children. Therefore, if a client desires the image of a happy unicorn, a dizzy elephant, or a laughing dinosaur, Weichers is often the tattoo artist of choice. As she explains, "There is a style of drawing and tattooing that I did come up with . . . called 'whims.' They are these little child-like drawings that I do. They're very whimsical and people either get the humor or they don't . . . but their main purpose is to make people smile. Also people usually get them on a whim, hence their name."[24]

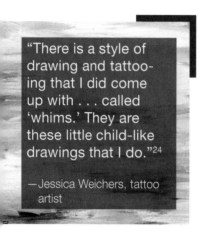

"There is a style of drawing and tattooing that I did come up with . . . called 'whims.' They are these little child-like drawings that I do."[24]

—Jessica Weichers, tattoo artist

Martian Architecture

Tattoo clients will not see dizzy elephants or happy unicorns on their bodies after a session with the Los Angeles–based tattoo artist known as Roxx. Tattooing in black ink only, Roxx favors geometric patterns—hexagons, circles, and triangles linked by common lines—that encircle her clients' bodies. Journalist Chris Gayomali states that "Roxx's organic geometry style stands out immediately. She does huge tapestries of black work, with complicated geometric patterns that look more like Martian architecture than body art."[25]

40

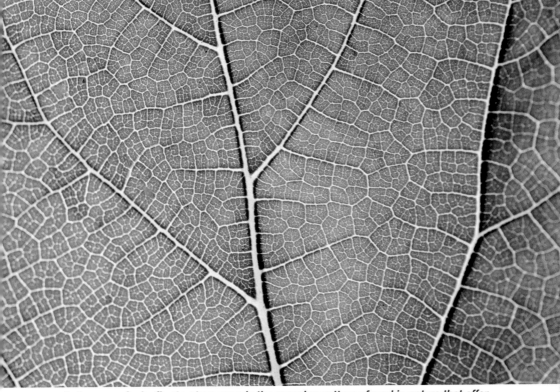

A close-up of a leaf's structure reveals the complex patterns found in nature that offer inspiration to many artists, including the tattoo artist Roxx, who is drawn to nature's simple, clean lines and geometric shapes.

In fact, Roxx says she is inspired by nature, although she acknowledges that her inspiration does not come from landscapes of green valleys or seascapes of rolling ocean waves. Rather, Roxx says she takes her inspiration from nature at its most basic form: the molecules and cells that make up living things.

Roxx says she developed her style after years of rendering tattoos mostly in realism. As she worked in that style, though, Roxx says she found beauty in the lines and shapes that made up the images. Thus, she began honing her style, breaking down the images into the geometric shapes that are at their core. She says,

I started really whittling things down to really simplistic shapes. I really got into the forms for the sake of geometry, things woven from the fabric of nature. . . . It's taking things down to a microscopic level. The structure of leaves and shells—basically just looking deeper into the molecular things that things are made up of. Seeing the repeating patterns and the geometry, the stuff that's always fascinated mystics and philosophers and shamans; how to make sense of the universe. It's about the puzzles of things. It kind of just never ends up getting boring. You go deeper and deeper into it.[26]

Inspiration Finds Them

Artists like Roxx and Weichers can cite specific forms of inspiration, whether they are geometric patterns, storybook characters, or the artwork of Giger or Dürer. But it is also true that many tattoo artists do not look for inspiration; rather, they hope inspiration finds them. For example, tattoo artist Alison Manners says she counts on her clients to provide her with inspiration. Based in Brisbane, Australia, Manners says she confers closely with her clients, first learning their desires, then working with them to provide images they find appealing. Her clients have left her studio bearing images of hawks spreading their wings across a chest, mermaids frowning across a forearm, and squawking birds perched atop an abdomen. She works in both color and black ink. Customers who want an image of a skull, kewpie doll, or peace symbol can find it in her flash art. "I make what I see in my head," she says. "What I think is beautiful."[27]

"I started really whittling things down to really simplistic shapes. I really got into the forms for the sake of geometry, things woven from the fabric of nature."[26]

—Roxx, tattoo artist

Los Angeles–based tattoo artist Paul Timman, whose clients include Hollywood stars Angelina Jolie, Ben Affleck, and Mark Wahlberg, suggests that inspiration often takes artists by surprise. Asked where he finds inspiration, he says, "From everything . . . from pillow cases to tissue boxes, to women's dresses to napkins, to menus to graffiti, to modern art to other tattoo artists.

Tattoos Inspired by Graffiti

Graffiti is a form of outdoor art applied to walls and other public spaces. Artists often render bold, cartoonish images, using cans of spray paint to create colorful depictions of characters and events. Graffiti is often applied illegally because artists typically do not bother to obtain permission from property owners before they create their images.

In 1999 Ninne Oat got his start in the art world by painting illegal graffiti. He has since given up graffiti and now creates tattoos at a studio in the city of Nicosia on the Mediterranean island of Cyprus. Oat brings the slashing style of the graffiti artist to his work on his clients' skin. "Initially his tattoo designs were not the same as the work he did on walls . . . but as time went on it intertwined into a consistent style of character design," says Adriana De Barros, the editor of the arts magazine *Scene360*. "Through his characters Ninne Oat depicts lonely souls, however, there is still lightheartedness to them."

Oat's body art features faces with bulging eyes and tongues hanging out of their mouths, pompous gentlemen with oversized mustaches, stern-faced women with dangling earrings, but also lovable pooches and other animals. He says, "I am inspired by love and I live my life in a positive way, so 'humor' couldn't be missing [from my work]."

Adriana De Barros, "From Graffiti to Tattooing: The Body Art of Ninne Oat," *Scene360*, August 19, 2018. https://scene360.com.

Quoted in De Barros, "From Graffiti to Tattooing."

Anything that catches my eye. That's where everyone gets it from. Everyone subconsciously takes something from everything and goes with it, everything inspires me."[28]

And sometimes, Timman concedes, the inspiration simply is not there:

> There are days where I have sent clients home as I was drawing on their [arms] waves or flames. . . . It wasn't flowing the way that I wanted it to, or it wasn't producing what I wanted . . . [so I told them] "we're not doing this

today" and I send them home. The next day when they come back you can draw it on in twenty seconds and it clicks, it's perfect. So you never know how it's going to go. Artists are artists, we are finicky people and that's just how it goes.[29]

Clearly, the era when the Bowery tattoo artists could render virtually identical images on the arms of the hundreds of sailors who sat in their chairs is long over. Tattooing is now a form of art that depends largely on the individual inspirations and talents of the artists. Schinkel is inspired by the hideous space creatures created by Giger, but artists like Middleton and Weichers find inspiration in much friendlier creatures. Betts is enthralled with the actual lettering that helps tell the story of a tattoo, firmly believing that the tattoo's message can be enhanced by the shape and size of the typeface that accompanies the image. And Roxx breaks down images into their simplest geometric patterns. These different styles illustrate the fact that each artist approaches the art of tattoo from his or her own deeply individual and personal perspective.

CHAPTER FOUR

Creating a Following

Kat Von D got her first piece of body art in 1996 at the age of fourteen—the letter *J* tattooed on her ankle. She was so enamored with tattoo art and culture that she dropped out of high school with the dream of becoming a professional tattoo artist. She soon found an apprenticeship in Los Angeles at Sin City Tattoo, where her artistic talent and style quickly flourished.

In the more than two decades since first picking up a tattoo needle, Kat Von D—her full name is Katherine Von Drachenberg—has opened her own tattoo studio, High Voltage Tattoo in West Hollywood, California. She has also starred in two television reality shows about tattoo culture—*Miami Ink* and *LA Ink*. She has written three best-selling books about her life in the tattoo world, created her own cosmetics and clothing lines, and occasionally acted in television shows and films. Her celebrity tattoo clients have included pop stars Miley Cyrus, Sebastian Bach, Ville Valo, Dave Navarro, and Travis Barker; actor-singer Eric Balfour; actors Nicole Richie, Mira Sorvino, and Stephen Baldwin; and comedian Margaret Cho, among others.

Looking back on her career, Kat Von D says her big break came in 2005 when she was recruited for the cast of *Miami Ink* on the TLC network. She was working at a Los Angeles tattoo studio at the time and received a call from a friend, tattoo artist Chris Garver, who was part of the *Miami Ink* cast. The producers of the show wanted to add a female artist to the cast and invited her to Miami for an audition. The show, which was based at the

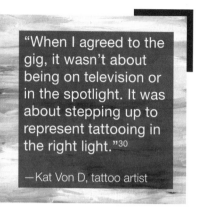
tattoo studio 305 Ink, located in the hip Miami neighborhood known as South Beach, aired the true-life trials of the artists: their conflicts and friendships with one another as well as their interactions with their clients. Kat Von D says she accepted the offer reluctantly because she feared that if she failed, her poor performance would cast a negative light on the art of tattooing and, in particular, the competence of female tattoo artists. Nonetheless, she says, she wanted to be sure that women were well represented. She explains,

> The thought of an inexperienced female tattooer misrepresenting everything I had been working so hard for made me sick to my stomach. When I agreed to the gig, it wasn't about being on television or in the spotlight. It was about stepping up to represent tattooing in the right light. The whole thing happened practically overnight. . . . I was greeted at the Miami airport by a few people from the production crew, and the sound guy rushed to wire me with a mic. The cameras rolled, documenting my every move and twitch, from picking up my luggage and getting a cab to arriving on set at the South Beach shop.[30]

Social Media Helps Build Brands

As things turned out, of course, Kat Von D emerged as a star and helped prove women can be talented tattoo artists and become leaders in a profession that has been dominated for more than a century by men. And there is no question that her celebrity has helped boost the public perception of tattoos as art. *Inked* magazine writer Devon Preston says, "Kat Von D has one of the most successful and profitable brands of any tattoo artist in history. Not only was she able to make a name for herself in the industry as an artist, but she created a hugely successful makeup line. . . . Seriously, is there anything that Kat can't do?"[31]

Indeed, lest anybody doubt Kat Von D's popularity, one need only look at her social media following: by 2019, her Instagram account reported more than 7 million followers. She is followed on Twitter by more than 2 million fans and by more than 12 million on Facebook.

Social media has, in fact, emerged as an important way for tattoo artists to gain recognition—and not only for megastars like Kat Von D. Certainly, few artists have the following that Kat Von D

Kat Von D takes a selfie with fans while promoting her makeup line. She has built a highly profitable brand and is considered a leader in a profession that has been largely dominated by men.

has earned; nevertheless, virtually all tattoo artists now regularly post their best work on their Instagram pages and on other social media sites.

Tea Leigh, a New York City–based tattoo artist, doubts her business could survive without Instagram. Leigh, who had more than fifty thousand followers on Instagram in 2019, estimates that 70 percent of her clients discover her work through the social media site. She says, "I want to use my follower base as a platform for anyone that I can; for me, that's the sole purpose of Instagram. Part of my personal brand is promoting the art that I want other people to know about."[32]

Tattoos on Television

After Kat Von D starred on *Miami Ink* in 2005, dozens of other tattoo artists found their talents in demand by TV producers. Since the debut of *Miami Ink*, more than twenty cable reality shows have featured the trials and talents of tattoo artists. Among them are *Ink Master, NY Ink, Tattoo Titans,* and *Epic Ink.* The scenarios for the shows are similar: camera crews follow artists as they interact with coworkers and clients. Some shows feature competitions among tattoo artists who vie for lucrative cash prizes.

After the season ends, many of the tattoo artists return to their normal lives. Some find the shows have helped boost their careers, although none has enjoyed the fame that Kat Von D has achieved. More typical is the experience of Pittsburgh tattoo artist Sarah Miller, who competed on *Ink Master* in 2012, finishing as first runner-up. Thanks to the celebrity she achieved on *Ink Master*, Miller went on a worldwide tour, appearing at numerous tattoo conventions. In 2014 she was approached by the television network Spike to star in the show *Ink Shrinks*. On the show, she helped troubled clients find healing through tattoo art. "As a tattoo artist, we already are basically therapists," says Miller. "Clients come in, sit with us, tell us their problems and we're able to give a spin on it that will help them or give some advice or a sympathetic ear." Ultimately, *Ink Shrinks* ran for a single season on Spike.

Quoted in *Inked*, "Meet Your New Ink Shrink: Sarah Miller," December 16, 2014. www.inkedmag.com.

And since Instagram and other social media sites give artists a chance to post more than just their flash and photos of their finished tattoos—such as information on their backgrounds as artists as well as the feedback they receive from clients—potential clients can use the sites to learn more about the artists before they commit themselves to a session under the tattoo needle. "I think people want a more personal experience when it comes to getting tattoos," says New York City tattoo artist Erika Kenia. "As an artist, Instagram allows you to share more of yourself and give your followers a peek behind the curtain. . . . Being able to relate to the artist on another level makes their work that much more collectible."[33]

"As an artist, Instagram allows you to share more of yourself and give your followers a peek behind the curtain."[33]

—Erika Kenia, tattoo artist

Websites and Live Streams

Artists like Leigh and Kenia make use of the Internet in other ways as well. Both artists maintain their own websites where they provide biographies and examples of their work. Other tattoo artists regularly produce videos and post them on YouTube and Vimeo. California tattoo artist Robin Hernandez—known to his followers as Lil B—has created a YouTube channel with more than two hundred thousand subscribers. He uses the channel to showcase his work and answer questions posted by followers. Hernandez says he finds YouTube videos to be the most effective way to display his art. He explains,

The show is a vlog that my friends and I post on YouTube every Monday. . . . It's all about sharing positive energy and showing our vision of life [and] art. You know in this tattoo game I just felt like I never fit in. My approach and the way I moved was always different [from] what I was exposed to when I was learning to tattoo. . . . The fact [that I] don't belong to a certain crowd was frustrating but afterwards I realized that it was my strength and that we had something going on for ourselves: Something that was worth sharing with other people that might have felt the same way. We also started the show just to have fun. We never really took it as something very serious but things picked up and we ran with it.[34]

Another tattoo artist who posts his work on YouTube is Florin Zaharia, who renders tattoos from his studio in the Romanian city of Constanta. YouTube has given him a platform, enabling him to present his art to an international audience. By 2019, his YouTube channel had nearly three hundred thousand followers. Moreover, visitors to Zaharia's website can find videos of his past work and watch him applying tattoos while live streaming.

Giant Steps Away from the Bowery

Although social media and the wider Internet help tattoo artists attain recognition and showcase their art, tattoos cannot be applied online. The only way for a client to receive a tattoo is to walk into a studio and put himself or herself in the hands of the artist. Therefore, the actual application of the tattoo has not really changed that much since the days of the Bowery shops of a century ago.

But the studios themselves certainly have changed. A half century or more ago, tattoo studios were invariably housed in tiny spaces, most in back alleys rather than on main streets. The walls were covered in flash and the chairs were usually threadbare. Cleanliness was always a concern. In the twenty-first century, by contrast, many owners want their tattoo studios to reflect good taste and professionalism. At the Black Amethyst Tattoo Gallery in St. Petersburg, Florida, clients enter a studio decorated in stark black with violet curtains and tile floors. While waiting for their turn in the tattoo chair, they can browse through an art gal-

Mister Cartoon Spreads His Brand

One way in which tattoo artists can find success is to put their tattoo images on surfaces other than human skin. Perhaps no tattoo artist has found more success at spreading his brand than Mark Machado of Los Angeles, who tattoos under the name of Mister Cartoon.

Over the years, Machado has accumulated a long list of celebrity clients, among them Snoop Dogg, Beyoncé Knowles, Justin Timberlake, Bow Wow, Method Man, Eminem, 50 Cent, and Dr. Dre. Sportswear manufacturers such as Nike and New Era have featured his characters on their apparel. In 2018 clothing brand the Hundreds introduced a line of T-shirts, baseball hats, wool caps, hoodies, jackets, and other apparel featuring the tattoo characters created by Machado. Among his images are a hip-hop cat named Bronson, a smiling cannonball, a devilish clown, and a girl with long, flowing hair named Hunny. Machado also designed the logo and artwork that appears on the equipment of the Los Angeles Kings hockey team. "I did the helmets. The goalie's helmets. I hand-painted those," he says. "All their apparel, too. So, all the hoodies, t-shirts."

Quoted in Uproxx, "From Tattooing to Car Customization, Mister Cartoon Explains It All," August 27, 2013. https://uproxx.com/viral/mister-cartoon-smoking-sessions-interview.

lery on the premises as well as a clothing boutique. Mule Tattoo in Tustin, California, favors an Old West look, with exposed brick walls, leather furniture, and tiny statuettes of mules placed around the studio. At Black Lotus Tattoo in Hanover, Maryland, clients encounter a reception area with long, cushioned sofas that sit atop a shiny hardwood floor. They may browse through the studio's art gallery or relax by playing Xbox video games.

Perhaps no tattoo studio has taken as many giant steps away from the old-fashioned, back-alley shops as Bang Bang, which operates two studios in New York City. A Bang Bang studio features marble floors and countertops, with tasteful lighting hanging overhead. The walls are decorated with art. Television screens hang in the reception room, showing videos of Bang Bang artists at work. (The videographer who produces the films is a full-time Bang Bang employee.) A wall in one of the studios houses an immense aquarium, where colorful koi fish entertain the clients. If clients prefer, they may wait for their appointments in downstairs lounges where expensive bottled waters are sold. Clients have included pop musicians Miley Cyrus, Demi Lovato, Katy Perry, Justin Bieber, and Rihanna; actor Michael J. Fox; and football stars Cam Newton and Odell Beckham Jr.

There is no question that owner Keith McCurdy—who tattoos under the nickname "Bang Bang"—has made Bang Bang into one of the preeminent tattoo studios in the world by hiring the best talent, including Eva Karabudak. But along with the talented artists, the posh studios, and the celebrity endorsements comes the hard reality that the tattoos produced at Bang Bang are perhaps the most expensive in America, if not the world. A junior tattoo artist at the studio earns no less than $400 an hour—and most tattoos take more than a single hour. And the top artists, such as Karabudak, are likely to charge much more. (According to the website AuthorityTattoo, $100 to $150 an hour is the typical price range charged by most tattoo artists in America.)

A sleeve, which is a tattoo that covers virtually the entire arm of the client, is likely to require several sessions in the chair and cost as much as $20,000. One of Bang Bang's artists, Jonathan Valena, who is known as JonBoy and whose clients have included Kendall Jenner, Travis Scott, Zayn Malik, and Hailey Baldwin, says clients would do well to remember they are buying body art that will be with them for a lifetime. "Tattoos are on you forever and you essentially get what you pay for," he says. "Good tattoos aren't cheap and cheap tattoos aren't good."[35]

Tattoo Conventions

Whether tattoo artists charge $100 an hour or $400, chances are many of them enjoy showing off their work at the numerous tattoo conventions staged annually in many American cities. Held in large conference centers or sports arenas, the conventions fea-

A "sleeve," a tattoo that covers virtually the entire arm, requires many sessions with an artist and can cost thousands of dollars.

ture tattoo artists giving tattoos to convention attendees. Many tattoo artists show off their flash, as well as merchandise such as T-shirts, hoodies, baseball caps, and posters displaying their work. The conventions also frequently feature well-known tattoo artists who give lectures about their art and provide demonstrations.

Tattoo artist Alan Chen, who participated in the 2018 Chicago Tattoo Arts Convention, said tattoo conventions illustrate how the art has progressed since the days of the back-alley shops. He told a reporter that tattooing is out in the open, performed in some of the biggest convention venues in America. "It's great

An artist is at work during a tattoo convention in Poland. Convention goers can get tattoos and meet their favorite artists, and tattoo artists can network, display their flash art, and sell merchandise.

that it's going mainstream and people can make a living with their art,"[36] he says. Meanwhile, at the Chicago convention tattoo artist Leeuh Vandever was busy rendering a tattoo of a flower on a walk-in client's hip. She acknowledged to a reporter that a lot of her work lately has focused on providing clients with tattoos of flowers on their hips and legs. "The hip and thigh area is becoming a really popular spot for flowers," she said. "That's definitely a trend I've been picking up on."[37]

Tattoo conventions, as well as social media, television reality shows, and upscale tattoo studios, all illustrate how the tattoo business has changed since the days of the Bowery. This modern culture of tattoo art was no doubt responsible for helping to make Kat Von D into an international superstar. Other tattoo artists may never reach that degree of fame; nevertheless, the acceptance of tattoo art by a large proportion of the public is likely to guarantee their success for years to come.

CHAPTER FIVE

The Future of Tattoo Art

Quick response (QR) codes are essentially barcodes that were first employed during the 1990s to help factories keep track of parts as they move through the manufacturing process. QR codes are tiny black-and-white squares that—when passed across an optical scanner—provide information that can be interpreted by a computer. QR codes have also been put to consumer use. For example, magazine readers who see QR codes printed on the pages are usually invited by the text to hold their smartphone cameras above the codes, prompting videos to appear on their smartphone screens.

In 2011 Ballantine's, a liquor distillery, approached French tattoo artist Karl Marc to create a tattoo containing a QR code. The tattoo Marc applied to the chest of the volunteer client was designed as a commentary on technology, displaying cartoonish cogs, gears, and wheels. However, within the design was the QR code, which Marc had to meticulously render because if just one element of the black-and-white box was imperfect, the QR code would fail to respond. Ultimately, the tattoo was a success. After the body art was completed, Marc held a smartphone camera up to the tattoo, which sparked a short video on the phone's screen, showing a humorous animation of an opera singer performing an aria. Ballantine's eventually employed a video of Marc's work rendering a QR code within a tattoo in an advertising campaign.

Embedding a QR code into a tattoo illustrates the degree to which cutting-edge technology has already impacted tattoo art. Tattoos that store digital data, tattoos that are rendered in new

A young woman at a music festival in New York shows off her flash tattoo, a popular style of temporary tattoos that are growing in demand.

types of ink, and tattoos that are no longer even composed of ink are all expected to dominate the art in the future. As technology writer Adam Clark Estes explains, "A new era of tattoos essentially reinvents the very definition of the art by pushing the boundaries of technology."[38]

Looking Like Neon

Although tattooing in the twenty-first century is a much different art form than it was a hundred or even fifty years ago, in truth the technology behind the art has not changed dramatically since Samuel O'Reilly invented the tattoo machine in 1891. Even though many modifications have been made to the device over the past several decades, the ink is still applied to the dermis in much the same fashion as it was in the early days of the Bowery era.

But chemists looking at the ink that tattoo artists inject into their clients' skin are finding new formulations that may help enhance the art. For example, tattoos that glow under black light fluorescent bulbs were introduced during the 1990s. (These bulbs do not emit black rays of light; rather, the glow is violet. The black light rays are emitted in the ultraviolet, or UV, spectrum, which includes waves of light found in sunlight that are primarily responsible for the tanning process.) Objects treated with dyes and paints containing chemicals known as fluorophores, which absorb and reflect UV light, glow when exposed to black light. The chemical phosphorus is a fluorophore typically used in fluorescent tattoo ink.

Fluorescent inks have grown very popular among tattoo clients. Dance clubs and rave organizers often illuminate the dance floors with black light; therefore, dancers with fluorescent tattoos find themselves at the center of the action. "They like that they can go ahead and get a dragon done on their arm and have the UV ink put into the eyes or into the flames from the mouth," says William Scherbarth, a tattoo artist in Columbus, Wisconsin. "When you put them under the light, they almost look neon. They're very brilliant."[39]

"A new era of tattoos essentially reinvents the very definition of the art by pushing the boundaries of technology."[38]

—Adam Clark Estes, technology writer

The End of Tattoo Regret

Another change in the chemistry of tattoo ink involves the longevity of the ink itself—in other words, how long it remains in the dermis. Tattoos have always been essentially permanent. Certainly, they can be removed, but it is a long, painful, and expensive process that must be conducted not by a tattoo artist but by a dermatologist, which is a physician who specializes in treating skin disorders. Therefore, anybody who walks into a tattoo studio would do well to understand that the tattoo they walk out with will very likely be with them for life.

Nevertheless, buyer's remorse—in the world of body art, it is known as tattoo regret—is a major issue among many clients who have gotten tattoos. Perhaps they were tattooed with the name of a boyfriend or girlfriend, but the relationship eventually ended. Now, they find themselves stuck with tattoos they no longer want.

A patient undergoes laser tattoo removal, which is painful and costly. Semipermanent ink, which lasts from three months to a year, might be a better choice for some to prevent tattoo regret.

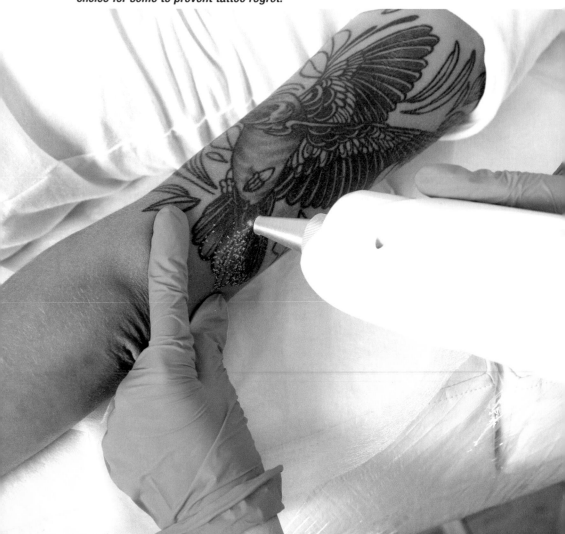

This happened to pop star Ariana Grande in 2018. After announcing her engagement to comedian Pete Davidson, she had the name *Pete* tattooed onto a finger. Months later, though, the couple broke up. Later that year, Grande was photographed with a bandage covering her finger. Celebrity gossip reporters speculated that Grande was either covering up the tattoo with the bandage or had it surgically removed and needed to keep the skin bandaged while it healed. Either way, Grande found herself tattooed with the name of a former boyfriend.

And Davidson faced the same problem. Shortly after the couple announced their engagement, Davidson had the French words *mille tendresse,* meaning "a thousand tendernesses," tattooed on the back of his neck. The celebrity gossip press reported that he chose those words to express his love for Grande. After the breakup, rather than surgically removing the script, he camouflaged it with a new and larger tattoo inked over it. The new tattoo consisted of a single word: *Cursed*. Clearly, both stars suffered through the pangs of tattoo regret.

Perhaps Grande and Davidson could have saved themselves considerable angst if they had gotten tattooed with a semipermanent ink that had been developed in 2018. This cutting-edge ink only lasts between three months and a year. Therefore, if the tattoo outlasts the relationship, the body art will eventually disappear. The technology was developed by graduates of New York University (NYU). They determined the reason tattoos last a lifetime is because the chemicals in the ink are packed into molecules that are too big to be attacked by the body's immune system. The answer was to reformulate the chemicals into smaller molecules. Then the client's antibodies—the natural chemicals in the body that attack and eliminate germs—can go to work on the ink molecules.

In the new formulation, it takes the antibodies just three months to a year to destroy all the molecules in the tattoo. When they have finished their work, the body art is gone. One of the NYU graduates who developed the process, Seung Shin, says he was inspired to explore disappearing tattoo ink after he got a tattoo and

The Future of Tattoo Removal

Getting a tattoo can be painful. After all, the typical tattoo requires thousands of pricks by a needle. Still, getting a tattoo is far less painful than getting rid of one. The most common method employed by physicians to remove tattoos is known as dermabrasion, in which the skin is shaved off with a device not unlike an electrical sander used in woodworking. Although numbing agents are used to ease the pain, the procedure still hurts a lot. Also, it is common for surgical scars to be left behind after the skin has healed.

In recent years, improvements have been made in tattoo removal through the use of lasers. In laser surgery, the skin is first numbed. A laser is then applied to the surface of the skin, shooting a laser pulse that shatters the embedded tattoo ink. Unlike dermabrasion, laser surgery is not likely to leave scars. However, several treatments may be needed, and the laser may not be able to remove an entire tattoo if the ink is dark and spread over a wide area. Moreover, laser surgery is no less painful than dermabrasion. Stephanie Holland, who works in a dermatology office in Phoenix, Arizona, offers this description: "Being hit with the laser feels like having hot bacon grease splashed on you while being simultaneously snapped with a thick rubber band."

Stephanie Holland, "Laser Technology Is Making Tattoo Removal Easier than Ever," *Smithsonian*, August 28, 2015. www.smithsonianmag.com.

then suffered tattoo regret, eventually having it removed through painful surgery. "Ever since I was young, I was always interested in tattoos but my parents were extremely against it, mostly because of its permanence,"[40] he says.

Robot Tattoo Artists

Whether the ink glows under black light or disappears within a year, it would still be applied in the old-fashioned way: by an artist using a tattoo machine. But that concept may change as well. The evolution of three-dimensional (3-D) printing that has helped revolutionize manufacturing during the first two decades of the twenty-first century may soon find its way into the tattoo studio.

In other words, in the future, the actual application of tattoos may become the job of a robot.

Three-dimensional printing is performed by a machine not unlike the conventional computer printer that churns out documents. A 3-D printer still follows commands transmitted by a computer, but instead of dispensing ink on a sheet of paper, the nozzle of the printer disgorges liquefied plastic, creating an object rather than a document. The liquefied plastic hardens as it emerges from the nozzle, creating a 3-D object layer by layer. Such printers are employed by industries to produce parts for equipment and by consumers who make gadgets for use around the house. In 2014, three French college students, Pierre Emm, Piotr Widelka, and Johan Da Silveira, modified a 3-D printer to dispense tattoo ink rather than liquefied plastic. They named the machine the Tatoué.

The human body has innumerable and unique curves, crevices, bumps, and other imperfections. Therefore, by scanning the body with a separate scanning device and feeding the scans into a computer, a 3-D printer would theoretically be far more capable than an artist holding a tattoo needle to apply the tattoo so it fits perfectly across the client's very imperfect body. The artist still has a role in the process: he or she designs the tattoo and then scans it into the computer. The printer then follows the design as the nozzle travels across the client's body. Emm, Widelka, and Da Silveira first tested the process on a piece of simulated skin; they then asked for volunteers at their university in Paris. Numerous student volunteers lined up, all eager to receive tattoos from the Tatoué. "A lot of people were excited by the idea of being the first human tattooed by a robot,"[41] says Emm.

> "A lot of people were excited by the idea of being the first human tattooed by a robot."[41]
>
> —Pierre Emm, robotics pioneer

Pouncing Tigers

If 3-D printers or similar robots eventually make their way into tattoo studios, at least they will still be using ink. Some researchers

61

are starting to wonder, though, whether people who want tattoos would be better off with a substance other than ink injected into their bodies. At the University of Pennsylvania in Philadelphia, researchers are looking into technology that may someday be used to create tattoos electronically by implanting an LED under the skin.

An LED, or light-emitting diode, is a device that provides illumination. The advantage that an LED holds over a traditional light bulb is that it can be installed on a very small platform. For use in a tattoo, the LED could be attached to a small, flexible sheet of silicon that can be surgically implanted under the skin. The LED could be programmed and operated remotely through a switching device that would cause it to be illuminated whenever the wearer wants to show off the design. The LED is powered by a tiny battery contained within the device. Moreover, many researchers believe it is possible to program the LED to display different designs. Therefore, it may be possible in the future to exhibit a tiger on Tuesday, a skull and dagger on Wednesday, and a hula dancer on Thursday. It may also be possible to use LED light sources to create animated tattoos. The tiger could pounce, for example, or the hula dancer could actually dance.

The University of Pennsylvania researchers experimenting with LED implants do not have tattoo art in mind for the devices. Instead, they think the science has much more potential for medical purposes, such as providing information on bodily functions to help doctors monitor symptoms in ill people. Still, the potential to use LED technology for tattoo art has captured the attention of the body-art community. Technology writer Charlie Sorrel says, "The first displays are sure to be primitive. . . . You won't be getting the full-color, hi-res images that come with ink, but functional displays."[42]

Interactive Tattoos

Another substance under examination for use in tattoo art—albeit temporary tattoo art—is known as DuoSkin. Unlike ink or LED devices, DuoSkin would be applied to the skin's surface rather

Tattoos and Augmented Reality

If smartphone owners want to play music on their devices, they have to go through the trouble of punching commands into their keypads. But now, a company in Los Angeles has created a tattoo that will take over that chore.

The company, Skin Motion, unveiled an app in 2017 that prompts a smartphone to start playing music simply by holding the device against one of its specially designed tattoos. To participate, a client downloads a tattoo design from the Skin Motion website. She or he then takes a printout of the design to a tattoo studio, where an artist uses it to make a stencil, guiding the creation of the tattoo.

Meanwhile, the client has uploaded music—or virtually any sound recording—to the Skin Motion cloud. After the tattoo is applied and the Skin Motion app is downloaded, the client can tap into a personal music library that can be accessed by exposing the smartphone to the tattoo. The technology is based on the concept of augmented reality, with the tattoo design containing perceptual information that can be interpreted by the smartphone app. In this case, the design tells the app to play music. Bryan Vangelder, a professional sound engineer who got a Skin Motion tattoo, explains that "the app matches the tattoo image to the sound you picked. That means anything can work: voicemails, love notes . . . anything your heart desires can be uploaded to the Skin Motion cloud."

Bryan Vangelder and Ariel Nunez, "Skin Motion App Turns My Tattoo into Sound Waves," CNET, March 13, 2018. www.cnet.com.

than injected into or implanted under the skin. More than just a removable decal, though, DuoSkin is composed of gold leaf that can be fashioned into an artistic design, often geometric patterns.

But DuoSkin has a far larger purpose than just providing the wearer with a decorative pattern: DuoSkin contains tiny circuit boards, meaning the tattoos can be interactive. When the wearer touches a spot on the DuoSkin surface, a television can be turned on or a channel can be changed, music can start playing, or a phone call can be made. In other words, DuoSkin can take the place of a television remote, a computer keyboard, or a cell phone keypad. As fashion writer Jess Edwards explains, "DuoSkin has created a new kind of tattoo. Not only do they look really pretty but they also will allow anyone to create interfaces directly on their skin, which basically means, your arm could soon become your computer keyboard. Which is pretty mind-blowing."[43] In 2019 DuoSkin remained under development in a joint project by engineers at the Massachusetts Institute of Technology (MIT) and software developer Microsoft.

DuoSkin can control remote devices for televisions and perhaps garage doors because the MIT and Microsoft engineers have found ways to enable these very thin gold-leaf tattoos to store and transmit electronic data. Gold leaf was employed as the material for the tattoos for a number of reasons. For starters, it is malleable, meaning it can be easily cut and shaped into artistic forms, and it can also be molded to fit the client's body. "DuoSkin tattoos are customizable—volunteers who tried them at MIT were able to design their own tattoos instead of purchasing a one-size-fits-all device,"[44] says technology writer Carmen Drahl. Gold is also a metal, which means it can conduct electricity—and for the tattoo to be able to control a television or a cell phone, there must be electric current running through the body art.

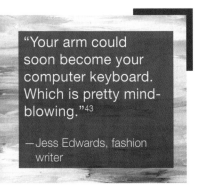

"Your arm could soon become your computer keyboard. Which is pretty mind-blowing."[43]

—Jess Edwards, fashion writer

Art in the Modern World

In the future, a person wearing a gold-leaf tattoo may be able to play a favorite song or start the microwave oven simply by touching a portion of the tattoo. Others may watch their tattoos come alive because the LED devices implanted under their skin are capable of projecting animations. Even if the science of tattoo art remains firmly covered in ink, changes are inevitable as well. Perhaps artists will be programming 3-D printers to apply

Jewelry-inspired temporary tattoos are a new style of body art that is dramatically different from the tattoo designs of the Bowery days.

the tattoos to their clients. Or their clients will be returning every few months for new tattoos because their old ones have been applied with disappearing ink.

Clearly, the art of tattoo in the future will look a lot different from the body art applied by such early pioneers as Sailor Jerry Collins and Lew Alberts. Tattoo art has already changed dramatically since the Bowery days. Artists with creativity and talent have come to dominate the field. As the future unfolds, new technology promises to take the art of tattoo even further, making it an important genre of art in the modern world.

$\mathcal{S}$OURCE NOTES

Introduction: Tattoo Art Joins the Mainstream

1. Steve Gilbert, *Tattoo History: A Sourcebook*. New York: Juno, 2000, p. 8.
2. Quoted in Carl Nolte, "Lyle Tuttle, Early Tattoo Artist, Leaves Indelible Mark on Society," *San Francisco Chronicle*, August 18, 2018. www.sfchronicle.com.
3. Joe Capobianco, "The Evolution of Tattoo Art," *Huffington Post*, December 6, 2017. www.huffingtonpost.com.

Chapter One: A Modern History of Tattoo Art

4. Brian Ashcraft with Hori Benny, *Japanese Tattoos: History, Culture, Design*. North Clarenton, VT: Tuttle, 2016, p. 139.
5. India Stoughton, "The Tattooed Hipsters of 18th-Century Japan," *Economist*, November 3, 2017. www.1843magazine .com.
6. Ashcraft, *Japanese Tattoos*, p. 9.
7. Gilbert, *Tattoo History*, p. 127.
8. Quoted in Emily Wilson, "Tattoo Legend 'Lew the Jew' Alberts Rediscovered at CJM," 48 Hills, July 30, 2018. https://48hills .org.
9. Anna Felicity Friedman, *The World Atlas of Tattoo*. New Haven, CT: Yale University Press, 2015, p. 25.
10. Friedman, *The World Atlas of Tattoo*, p. 27.

Chapter Two: Tattoo Artists of Influence

11. Quoted in Rebecca Harkins-Cross, "Hori Smoku Sailor Jerry: The Life of Norman K. Collins," *Beat*, 2019. www.beat.com.au.
12. Clinton R. Sanders with D. Angus Vail, *Customizing the Body: The Art and Culture of Tattoo*. Philadelphia: Temple University Press, 2008, p. 167.

13. Quoted in Ino Mei, "Filip Leu," *HeartbeatInk Tattoo Magazine*, 2019, no. 15. www.heartbeatink.gr.
14. Alex Wikoff, "Eva Krbdk's Emotionally Transportive Tiny Tattoos," Tattoodo, February 20, 2017. www.tattoodo.com.
15. Quoted in Zoe Schlanger, "3-D Tattoos Take Over," *Newsweek*, February 28, 2014, p. 1.
16. Quoted in *Inked*, "Yomico Moreno: Realism Tattoo Artist," January 10, 2017. www.inkedmag.com.
17. Quoted in Drew Grant, "Amanda Wachob: Portrait of a Tattoo Artist," *New York Observer*, December 16, 2016. https://observer.com.
18. Quoted in Grant, "Amanda Wachob."

Chapter Three: Inspirations Behind Tattoo Art

19. Quoted in Friedman, *The World Atlas of Tattoo*, p. 191.
20. Cyle Hoffman, *The Inked Book: The Tattoo Bible*. Middletown, DE: CreateSpace, 2017, p. 6.
21. Quoted in Friedman, *The World Atlas of Tattoo*, p. 91.
22. Quoted in Nick Schonberger, "The Complex Guide to Tattoo Lettering," Complex, September 12, 2011. www.complex.com.
23. *Inked*, "Yallzee's Amazing Lettering Tattoos," March 21, 2016. www.inkedmag.com.
24. Quoted in *Joey Voodoo* (blog), "Featured Tattoo Artist: Jessica Weichers," March 5, 2012. https://joeyvoodoo.wordpress.com.
25. Chris Gayomali, "Meet Roxx, the Woman at the Forefront of the Ink World's Coolest Artistic Movement," *GQ*, August 17, 2015. www.gq.com.
26. Quoted in Gayomali, "Meet Roxx, the Woman at the Forefront of the Ink World's Coolest Artistic Movement."
27. Quoted in Friedman, *The World Atlas of Tattoo*, p. 321.
28. Quoted in Emily Jolly, "Sculpture to Skin: How Paul Timman Made It Big in Hollywood," *HYPR*, August 9, 2018. https://hyprmagazine.com.
29. Quoted in Jolly, "Sculpture to Skin."

Chapter Four: Creating a Following

30. Kat Von D, *High Voltage Tattoo*. New York: HarperCollins, 2009, p. 15.

31. Devon Preston, "5 Tattoo Artists Who've Created Multi-Million Dollar Empires," *Inked*, November 8, 2018. www.inkedmag .com.

32. Quoted in Marian Bull, "How Instagram Has Indelibly Redrawn the Tattoo World," Daily Beast, February 16, 2016. www.the dailybeast.com.

33. Quoted in Taylor Bryant, "How Instagram Has Changed Tattoo Culture," Nylon, August 24, 2018. https://nylon.com.

34. Quoted in *Houseink*, "Lil B Tattoo," 2018. www.houseink .com.

35. Quoted in George Driver, "Everything You Need to Know Before Getting a Tattoo," *Elle*, August 23, 2017. www.elle.com.

36. Quoted in K.T. Hawbaker, "5 Things We Learned at the Chicago Tattoo Arts Convention," *Chicago Tribune*, April 3, 2018. www.chicagotribune.com.

37. Quoted in Hawbaker, "5 Things We Learned at the Chicago Tattoo Arts Convention."

Chapter Five: The Future of Tattoo Art

38. Adam Clark Estes, "The Freaky, Bioelectric Future of Tattoos," Gizmodo, January 6, 2014. https://gizmodo.com.

39. Quoted in *Milwaukee Journal Sentinel*, "Read Between the Lights: UV Tattoos," *Denver Post*, May 30, 2006. www .denverpost.com.

40. Quoted in David Nield, "This New Tattoo Ink Is Designed to Disappear After a Year," ScienceAlert, May 13, 2016. www .sciencealert.com

41. Quoted in Aviva Rutkin, "Permanent Tattoos Inked by Hacked 3D Printer," *New Scientist*, April 2, 2014. www.newscientist .com.

42. Charlie Sorrel, "The Illustrated Man: How LED Tattoos Could Make Your Skin a Screen," *Wired*, November 20, 2009. www .wired.com.

43. Jess Edwards, "DuoSkin Tattoos: The Metallic Tattoos That Double Up as a Touch Screen," *Cosmopolitan*, August 16, 2016. www.cosmopolitan.com.

44. Carmen Drahl, "The Surprisingly Simple Chemistry in Duo-Skin: Temporary Tattoos That Control Your Phone," *Forbes*, August 16, 2016. www.forbes.com.

*F*OR FURTHER RESEARCH

Books

Bang Bang, *Bang Bang: My Life in Ink*. New York: HarperCollins, 2015.

Tina Brown, *Tattoos: An Illustrated History*. Stroud, UK: Amberley, 2019.

Anna Felicity Friedman, *The World Atlas of Tattoo*. New Haven, CT: Yale University Press, 2015.

Andreas Johansson, *Yakuza Tattoo*. Årsta, Sweden: Dokument, 2017.

Jonathan Shaw, *Vintage Tattoo Flash: 100 Years of Tradition-al Tattoos from the Collection of Jonathan Shaw*. New York: PowerHouse, 2016.

Internet Sources

Marian Bull, "How Instagram Has Indelibly Redrawn the Tattoo World," Daily Beast, February 16, 2016. www.thedailybeast.com.

Joe Capobianco, "The Evolution of Tattoo Art," *Huffington Post*, December 6, 2017. www.huffingtonpost.com.

Chris Gayomali, "Meet Roxx, the Woman at the Forefront of the Ink World's Coolest Artistic Movement," *GQ*, August 17, 2015. www.gq.com.

Drew Grant, "Amanda Wachob: Portrait of a Tattoo Artist," *New York Observer*, December 16, 2016. https://observer.com.

David Nield, "This New Tattoo Ink Is Designed to Disappear After a Year," ScienceAlert, May 13, 2016. www.sciencealert.com.

Websites

Bang Bang Forever (www.bangbangforever.com). This website, maintained by New York City's most exclusive tattoo studios, provides visitors with a guided tour of the two Bang Bang studios, displaying the luxurious accommodations awaiting clients. The site also provides images of tattoos rendered by individual Bang Bang artists, including Eva Karabudak.

Inked (www.inkedmag.com). *Inked* is the tattoo world's most widely read magazine. Its website features interviews with top tattoo artists, photographs of cutting-edge tattoos, and updates on trends in the tattoo world, such as technological developments and artistic innovations. By accessing the link for "Culture," visitors can find stories about the influence of realism in tattoo art, clients who get their faces tattooed, and the latest celebrities who have gotten inked.

Inked Cartel (https://inkedcartel.com). Inked Cartel strives to display the most cutting-edge art in the tattoo world. Visitors to the website can find profiles of such leading tattoo artists as Kat Von D, Paul Timman, Lyle Tuttle, and Filip Leu. By following the link for "Tattoo Art," students can find photographs of numerous artistic styles, including realism, abstract renderings, styles of script, geometric patterns, and sailor-style body art.

Tattoo Archive (https://tattooarchive.com). Located in Winston-Salem, North Carolina, this tattoo studio's website includes numerous articles about the history of tattooing in America and elsewhere. Visitors can find stories about Samuel O'Reilly and the invention of the tattoo machine, the work of early artists such as Sailor Jerry Collins and Lew Alberts, and a history of Japanese tattooing.

Tattoodo (www.tattoodo.com). The website maintains a database of hundreds of tattoo artists, allowing visitors to see examples of their work while providing biographical information on the artists. Tattoodo also features articles on trends in tattoo art and reports from tattoo conventions. By following the television link, visitors can view short videos of tattoo artists at work.

*I*NDEX

$\mathcal{P}$ICTURE CREDITS

Cover: Mikhail_Kayl/Shutterstock.com

8: JStone/Shutterstock.com

12: akg-images/Newscom

17: Associated Press

21: Savanevich Viktar/Shutterstock.com

23: *Palm Beach Post*/ZUMAPRESS/Newscom

27: *The Kiss*, 1907–08 (oil on canvas), Klimt, Gustav (1862–1918)/Osterreichische Galerie Belvedere, Vienna, Austria/Bridgeman Images

31: Maddy Halpern

36: Everett Historical/Shutterstock.com

38: Scott Dumas/Shutterstock.com

41: SK Herb/Shutterstock.com

47: OFA/ZOJ/Oscar Gonzalez/WENN/Newscom

53: iStock.com/ClarkandCompany

54: De Visu/Shutterstock.com

56: Associated Press

58: New Africa/Shutterstock.com

65: Kristina Kokhanova/Shutterstock.com

Hal Marcovitz is a former newspaper reporter and columnist. He has written nearly two hundred books for young readers. His other book in the Art Scene series is *The Art of Graffiti*. He makes his home in Chalfont, Pennsylvania.